THE FORGOTTEN ARTS

Making Old-Fashioned
Pickles, Relishes, Chutneys, Sauces and Catsups, Mincemeats, Beverages and Syrups

One hundred and thirty-six treasured family
recipes, selected from the thousands submitted to
The Old Farmer's Almanac and *Yankee* Magazine

YANKEE BOOKS
Camden, Maine

Illustrated by Margo Letourneau

Designed by Carl F. Kirkpatrick

Cherry Pyron and Clarissa M. Silitch, Editors

This book has been prepared by the staff of

Yankee Publishing Incorporated

First Edition

Copyright 1978 by Yankee Publishing Incorporated

Printed in the United States of America

10 9 8 7

Library of Congress Catalog Card No. 78-54880

ISBN 0-911658-84-X

Contents

Foreword

No county fair is complete without rows of gleaming, rainbow-hued jars of home-canned pickles, relishes, chutneys and other condiments. Prizes at these events are usually given on sight alone, but every discriminating eater knows a special pickle or relish that only taste can judge and without which that certain meal is incomplete.

The art of preserving cucumbers and other vegetables and fruits is an old one, dating from earlier days when there were no fresh vegetables and meats during the long winter months, and appetites grew jaded from a steady diet of grains, salt meats and root cellar vegetables. Brined pickles, tasty treats from the dill crock, pepper relishes and apple chutneys still spark even everyday meals and add elegance to a dinner party. Dill pickles liven up the plainest hamburger and many consider the hot dog incomplete without relish. The bite of vinegar or the piquancy of a sweet-sour spiced peach gives taste buds a thrill and the crunch of a firm kosher dill can add texture to any meal.

1
Pickled
Vegetables
& Fruits

About Pickling in General

Pickles should be made from young, fresh, sound vegetables and fruits, quality vinegar and fresh, whole spices and herbs. Satisfactory pickled products are the result of quality ingredients, proper proportions and carefully followed recipes.

Fruits and vegetables to be pickled should be washed thoroughly with a vegetable brush under running water. Soil or any soft spots left on the vegetables may contain bacteria which can cause the pickles to spoil. Cucumbers for pickling whole may have about a half inch of the stem left on; be sure to remove the blossom ends of the cucumbers, for they contain an enzyme which can cause softening of the cucumbers during fermentation.

When choosing vegetables for pickling, select those that are nearly the same size so that the pickling rate will be uniform. If both old and fresh vegetables are used, the longer time required for processing the older vegetables may result in overprocessing of the fresher vegetables and a poor overall pickle.

Salt for pickling brines should be specifically canning or pickling salt — a pure, granulated or rock salt which has no iodine added — *not* iodized table salt. The iodine in table salt will darken pickles. Plain table salt may be used, but it contains anti-caking agents which will cloud the brine. Dairy salt or sea salt will also serve well for pickling purposes.

Vinegar is a common component of pickled products; it must have an acidity of 4 to 6 percent. The strength of vinegar is usually shown on the label. Since the acidity of homemade vinegar is hard to establish or may vary during the fermentation or storage time, commercial vinegars are safer to use for pickling. Wine vinegars do not do well for pickling either, for they will develop a mother, a gathering of yeast and other bacterial organisms, during fermentation.

Cider vinegar will give a fuller, richer-flavored pickle but will also add some color to the pickle. If a lighter color product is desired, as with pickled pears or onions, white distilled vinegar may be used. Cider vinegar imparts a mellower taste, white vinegar a sharper taste, but both serve equally well for pickling.

Use the exact proportions of vinegar called for in your recipe; the vinegar is important to the keeping quality of the pickle. If the syrup or brine tastes too sharp, do not decrease the amount of the vinegar, but rather add more sweetener until the taste is right.

The **sugar** called for in sweetened pickle products is usually white granulated sugar. Brown sugar is best used only in those recipes which specifically call for it. Honey may be substituted for sugar — use about half as much honey as sugar; taste the solution before adding to the jars and adjust to taste.

Spices in pickles are usually used whole, because ground spices may darken the pickle and cloud the syrup or brine. Use fresh spices; old spices lose their pungency and may give a dusty taste to the pickle. When using whole spices, such as cloves, stick cinnamon and the commercial mixed pickling spice, tie them in a cloth bag unless the recipe specifies that they be left free in the syrup.

Two exceptions to the whole spice rule: if turmeric is called for in a recipe, you will have to use this spice ground since it is usually unavailable whole. Ground mustard is another exception which will be specified in a recipe.

To prevent spoilage of garlic used to season pickles, blanch the cloves for about two minutes before storing in jars. Unblanched garlic should be removed from the brine before packing the pickles in the jar.

Some pickle recipes call for a **crisper,** usually alum. Alum can have a shriveling effect on the pickles and may leave a slight taste. Grape and cherry leaves will serve the same purpose without any side effects. Dill pickles especially benefit from the addition of these leaves.

Because of the extensive use of acids and salts in pickling, any **utensils** used for heating brines should be of unchipped enamelware, stainless steel, or glass. Copper, brass, galvanized, or iron utensils may react with the acids or salts and cause color changes or form undesirable chemical compounds. Containers for fermenting pickles should be earthenware crocks or stoneware jars, unchipped enamel-lined pans, large glass jars, bowls or casseroles. If the brine must be covered, use a large china dinner plate weighed down by a glass jar filled with water.

Stirring utensils should be stainless steel or wooden; tongs, a ladle and a funnel will be helpful when filling the jars. A food grinder is necessary for making relishes or other pickles requiring chopped or ground vegetables.

Pickles may be made by either the long or the short method. The long method is *brining,* a fermentation process that goes on for about three weeks, during which time the vegetables are cured to a desirable flavor not excessively sour, salty or spicy. During the brining period, the physical structure of the vegetable is changed. The salt in the curing solution draws the water out of the vegetable cells, leaving space for the absorption of the sugars, vinegar and spices added in the final stages of pickling. The natural moisture from the vegetables combines with the brine solution to form lactic acid, which then cures or preserves the vegetable. The scum which forms on the surface of the brine during fermentation contains wild yeasts, mold and bacteria which may weaken the brine's acidity; this scum *must* be skimmed off daily. The vinegar and other seasonings added after brining further preserve and flavor the pickle.

The skin of the brined pickle is tender and firm, the inside is uniformly translucent and tender and firm, not soft and mushy. Many dill pickles are made by this brining process and are worth the effort involved. Sauerkraut is cabbage brined by the same process.

The shorter method of pickling vegetables is called *fresh-pack* and usually involves a brining process lasting from a few hours to overnight. These pickles are more pungent than the long-brined ones, but the texture is just as good and the varieties are endless. With this method, the salt brine begins the softening process of the vegetable, and the vinegar solution preserves the pickle by replacing the natural moisture drawn out by the salt and firming the softened tissue.

Fruit pickles are usually packed whole and simmered in a spicy sweet-and-sour syrup. The color of the fruit is preserved, lending eye appeal.

Most pickles need some time to season after they are packed in jars; three to six weeks' storage will produce a more finely flavored pickle. Pickles should be stored in a dark, dry cool place where there is no danger of freezing. Too much light may cause the pickles to deteriorate and change color.

For best results, pickled products should be processed in a boiling water bath after being packed in clean, sterilized canning jars. This heat treatment will destroy organisms that might cause spoilage and inactivate the enzymes that could affect flavor, color and texture during storage.

When using the following table and also when processing other pickle products, start counting the processing time as soon as the filled jars are placed in actively boiling water; exceptions to this procedure are explained. The canner used for the water bath should be deep enough so that about an inch of water will cover the tops of the jars when placed on a low rack.

So that the boiling water may circulate freely around them, the jars should not touch each other or the sides of the pan.

The following table gives processing times for vegetable and fruit pickles, sauerkraut and mincemeat. Correct processing times for the relishes, chutneys, catsups and sauces are given in those chapters. All processing times given are for elevations less than 1000 feet. For every additional 1000 feet of elevation, add 1 minute to the processing times given.

VEGETABLE PICKLES	PROCESSING TIME
	pint or quart
Jerusalem Artichoke Pickles	10
Beans, Green or Wax	5
Bread and Butter Pickles	10
Carrot Pickles	10
Dill Pickles, Brined	15
Dill Pickles, Fresh-Pack	20
Gherkin Pickles	5
Mustard Pickles	10
Onions	5
Peppers	5
Ripe Cucumber Pickles	5
Sour Pickles	5
Sweet Pickles	5
Tomato Pickles, Green or Ripe	10
Zucchini Pickles	10

FRUIT PICKLES

Fig Pickles	10
Hepzibah's Fruit Pickle	10
Maple Sweet Pickles	10
*Peaches	20
*Pears	20
Pineapple	10
Walnut	10
Watermelon	5

SAUERKRAUT

Brined or In-the-Jar	*pint* 15
	quart 20

MINCEMEAT

   Mincemeat made with beef and suet *must* be processed under pressure to assure safe keeping. Quarts of prepared mincemeat should be processed under 10 pounds of pressure for 25 minutes and stored in a dark, dry cool place for several weeks to season. Green tomato mincemeat does *not* require pressure processing if it has no beef or suet; it may be processed in a boiling water bath for 20 minutes.

*Start counting processing time as soon as water *returns* to boil.

To Be Avoided

If careful control is exercised over the pickling ingredients, utensils and procedures, many potential problems may be avoided. However, should inferior pickles reward your efforts, check the following list for possible explanation.

Soft or slippery pickles: too little salt or acid in brine; scum in brining process not removed regularly; cucumbers not covered with brine; too warm storage temperature; insufficient processing; blossom ends not removed from cucumbers.

Hollow pickles: poorly developed cucumbers; cucumbers left too long between harvest and pickling; improper strength brine during fermentation.

Shriveled pickles: allowing too much time between gathering and pickling; pickling solution too sweet or too strong in vinegar; brine too salty at beginning of curing (best to begin with dilute solution and gradually increase strength); overcooking or overprocessing of pickle.

Dark pickles: use of ground spices or too much spice; use of iodized salt; minerals in water, especially iron; use of iron utensils; overcooking.

Poorly colored or faded pickles: poor quality cucumbers; sunburned or overmature fruit.

Spoilage in sauerkraut is indicated by undesirable color (pinkish or gray), off odors and soft texture. Following are some specific indications of spoilage and their causes.

Soft kraut: insufficient salt; too high temperatures during fermentation; uneven distribution of salt; air pockets in jar due to improper packing.

Pink kraut: indicates yeast growing on surface of kraut; too much or unevenly distributed salt; kraut improperly covered or weighed down during fermentation.

Rotted kraut: cabbage not covered by brine on surface to exclude air during fermentation.

Dark kraut: unwashed and improperly trimmed cabbage; insufficient brine to cover fermenting cabbage; uneven distribution of salt; exposure to air during fermentation; high temperatures during fermentation, processing and storage; too long storage time.

Cucumbers

To most people, pickles mean pickled cucumbers. There are pickling varieties of cucumbers which make better pickles than those meant for slicing. *Pickling cucumbers are stockier and squarer, usually have a more warty exterior and a firmer interior which stays sounder when pickled. Small to medium-size cucumbers, 4 to 5 inches long, are a good size for whole pickles. For gherkins, use cucumbers 1-1/2 to 3 inches long. Cucumbers too large to be used whole may be quartered or sliced. The spears made from cutting cucumbers into fourths or eighths pack easily into canning jars and are attractive on the relish plate.*

Cucumbers are best for pickling when used immediately after harvesting; if they must wait to be processed, store them in the refrigerator, for they deteriorate rapidly at room temperature. However, the longer they are stored, even in the cold, the greater the tendency for them to make hollow, inferior pickles. Do not use cucumbers with wax on them; the brine cannot penetrate the wax. When adding the liquid to the jars of packed pickles, leave 1/2 inch headspace. For processing methods and times, see the Table on page 10.

processor

SPICY BREAD AND BUTTER PICKLES

1 gallon cucumbers, sliced	2 green peppers, shredded
8 small onions, shredded	1/2 cup salt

Mix thoroughly, cover with cubes of ice and let stand for 3 hours. Drain.

Add to the above mixture a syrup made by combining:

5 cups sugar	5 cups vinegar
1-1/2 teaspoons turmeric	2 whole cloves
2 tablespoons mustard seed	1 teaspoon celery seed

Heat to the boiling point but do not boil. Bottle and process. (See Table on page 10.) Makes 4 to 5 quarts.

BREAD AND BUTTER PICKLES WITH RED PEPPER

5 cups sliced cucumbers	1 green pepper, seeded and sliced
1 large onion (or 2 medium)	1 red pepper, seeded and sliced

Cover with 8 cups water and 4 tablespoons salt. Let stand 3 hours and then drain.

Cover with:

1 pint vinegar	1/2 teaspoon turmeric
1 cup brown sugar	1/2 teaspoon celery seed
1 teaspoon mustard seed	

Boil until clear. Bottle and process. (See Table on page 10.) Makes about 2 quarts.

MOLLIE'S BREAD AND BUTTER PICKLES

6 large cucumbers, sliced	1/4 cup salt
4 onions, sliced	

Let stand 1 hour and drain.
Heat:

1 pint white vinegar	1 teaspoon celery seed
3/4 cup sugar	1 teaspoon mustard seed

Cook the mixture for 3 minutes after the sugar has dissolved. Put vegetables in jars, pour in hot syrup, process immediately (see Table, page 10) and cool. Makes about 2 quarts.

SMALL SWEET CUCUMBER PICKLES

Wash 300 small cucumbers; wipe dry and lay in crock. Take 2/3 cup salt and sprinkle over the cucumbers. Then turn a kettle of boiling water over them to cover the cucumbers. Let stand overnight. In the morning remove from the brine, wipe each pickle dry and lay in a crock. Then take 1/2 gallon cold vinegar and mix it with 4 tablespoons dry mustard, the same of salt and sugar and cover the pickles with 1/2 cup mixed pickling spice and lay in a small root of ginger. Pour the mixture over the pickles and stir so each pickle is covered. Set away in a cool place. Weigh out 3 lbs. sugar and each morning add just a handful of sugar to the crock, stirring well, until the whole 3 lbs. has been used. After the last of the sugar is added, pack the cucumbers in quart jars and fill with cold vinegar from the crock. Do not heat the vinegar. Leave some of the mixed spice in each jar and put on covers. Process according to the Table on page 10. This is not half as much trouble as it sounds. Use cucumbers 2 to 2-1/2 inches long. If you do not have the number of cucumbers designated, then take what you have and divide other ingredients proportionately.

NINE-DAY SWEET PICKLES

4-5 dozen medium-size pickling cucumbers
1 gallon water
1 cup salt

Make a brine with the salt and water and cover the cucumbers with it. Let the cucumbers stand in the brine for 3 days. Drain off the brine and cover the cucumbers with boiling water. Let stand 2 hours, then pour off the water. Slice the cucumbers and cover with:

1 tablespoon alum dissolved in
1 gallon water

Let this stand 24 hours, then drain and cover again with a solution of:

1 gallon boiling water
1 pint white vinegar
1 teaspoon alum

Let this stand for another 24 hours. Drain. Make a pickling syrup of:

6 cups sugar
6 cups vinegar
2 tablespoons mixed pickling spice tied in a cloth bag

Heat this syrup, with the spice bag, to boiling. Pour the boiling syrup over the cucumbers. Each day for the next 3 days, drain the syrup from the cucumbers and heat it to boiling, adding

1 cup of sugar each day (3 cups in all)

After adding each day's cup of sugar, pour the boiling syrup back over the cucumbers. After these 3 days, pack the cucumber slices into jars, add

1 cup sugar

to the pickling syrup, heat the syrup, and pour over the packed cucumber slices. Process according to the Table on page 10.

SWEET RIPE CUCUMBER PICKLE

4 quarts ripe cucumbers
1 pint vinegar
4 cups sugar
1-inch stick cinnamon

Cut the cucumbers in chunks. Soak overnight in salted water (2 tablespoons salt to each quart of water). Drain. Boil the sugar and vinegar together until syrupy. Add cinnamon and cucumber chunks and cook until tender and transparent. Bottle and process. (See Table on page 10.) Makes about 4 quarts.

SLICED CUCUMBER PICKLE

1 quart green cucumbers, sliced
1 green pepper, chopped fine
3 sliced onions
1 cup sugar

1 teaspoon turmeric
1 teaspoon mustard seed
a few whole cloves
vinegar

Cover the vegetables with salt and let stand 3 hours. Drain well and add the sugar and spices. Cover with vinegar and heat through but do not boil. When just at the boiling stage, remove from the fire and bottle and process. (See Table on page 10.)

PICKLED GHERKINS

These are more than good!

Wash little gherkin cucumbers and pack tightly into cold jars. To 1 gallon of good strong cider vinegar, add 1 cup salt. Thoroughly dissolve and fill pickle jars to within 1/2 inch of top. Put on jar lids and process. (See Table on page 10.)

SOUR CUCUMBER PICKLES

1 gallon vinegar
1 cup sugar
1 cup salt

1 cup dry mustard
1 peck (10 lbs.) cucumbers

Mix the vinegar, sugar, salt and mustard thoroughly and put into a 5-gallon crock. Pick, wash, and wipe the cucumbers. Put them in the mixture. They will be ready for use in a few days and will keep indefinitely in the crock or may be packed in sterilized jars and processed (see Table on page 10) for storage.

MRS. PENTLAND'S PICKLES

A long-brined pickle.

Into a 5-gallon crock put:
1 gallon cider vinegar
1/2 cup onion, cut up
1/2 cup dry mustard

1/2 cup whole black peppercorns
4 4-inch pieces stick cinnamon
4 tablespoons whole cloves
1/2 cup salt

With a dry cloth, wipe small, whole cucumbers to clean and remove the spines; do not wash. Add the cleaned cucumbers to the vinegar mixture until the crock is full. Place a dinner plate over the cucumbers and brine to keep the cucumbers submerged; weigh down the plate with a clean quart jar filled with water. Every day skim the surface of the brine and then stir with a wooden spoon. Keep in a cool place. These will be ready to eat in 3 weeks.

BRINED DILL PICKLES

half bushel (about 20 lbs.)
  3- to 6-inch cucumbers
3/4 cup mixed pickling spice
3 bunches dill weed

2-1/2 cups vinegar
1-3/4 cups salt
2-1/2 gallons water

Wash the cucumbers thoroughly, being careful to remove all blossom ends, and wipe dry. Put half the pickling spice and a generous layer of dill on the bottom of a 5-gallon crock. Lay in the cucumbers to within 3 inches of the crock's top. Put a layer of dill and the remaining pickling spice on top of the cucumbers. Combine the vinegar, salt and water and pour over the cucumbers and spice.

Cover with a dinner plate and weigh this down with a water-filled jar. Be sure all the cucumbers are beneath the brine. Keep the crock at about 70°F for 3 weeks, skimming off the scum from the brine every day. Do not stir the pickles; if more brine is needed to cover the fermenting cucumbers, make additional brine using the original proportions of vinegar, salt and water.

After the 3 weeks, remove the pickles from the brine and pack, along with dill from the crock, in sterilized quart jars. Avoid too tight a pack. Strain the brine from the crock and heat to boiling. Fill the jars to within 1/2 inch of the top and process. (See Table on page 10.) Makes 9 to 10 quarts.

If a fresh brine is preferred over the brine from the crock, which may be a bit cloudy because of the fermentation process, prepare a canning brine by mixing 1/2 cup salt and 4 cups vinegar to 1 gallon of water. The brine from the crock may be preferred, despite its cloudiness, because of the added flavor.

FRESH KOSHER STYLE DILL PICKLES

30-36 cucumbers (3 to 4 inches
  long)
3 cups vinegar
3 cups water

6 tablespoons salt
fresh or dried dill
garlic
mustard seed

Wash the cucumbers. Bring to a boil a brine made with the vinegar, water and salt. Place a generous layer of dill (seed heads, leaves and stems are all suitable), 1/2 to 1 clove garlic, sliced and blanched, and 1/2 tablespoon of mustard seed in the bottom of a sterilized quart jar. Pack cucumbers vertically into half the jar, then add more dill and complete the jar with cucumbers. Fill the jars to within 1/2 inch of the top with the boiling brine. Cap and process (see Table on page 10). These pickles may shrivel after the processing but they will later plump in the sealed jars.

THE DILL CROCK

The old general store's pickle barrel finds a home version in the dill crock, a savory brine in a large stoneware or earthenware crock which in its depths mysteriously turns common garden vegetables into tangy, soul-satisfying pickles. A treat for family and visitor alike, the crock can work right in the kitchen from July through September, offering excellent relishes, hot summer afternoon refreshers and bedtime snacks.

Stoneware crocks range in size from as small as one quart to as large as twenty gallons. The five-gallon size is adequate for pickling, not too heavy to move when full and does not take up much storage space. In some areas, crocks may be hard to come by; practical substitutes, although not as traditional, are large glass crocks, wide-mouth gallon jugs and enameled preserving kettles.

Here's how to make your own dill crock.

Make a brine in the crock using the proportions of 1 gallon water, 1 gallon cider vinegar and 1 cup pickling salt. If you like the flavor, toss in a few garlic cloves. Pack in clean, fresh vegetables alternately with fresh dill weed, using heads, stems and leaves, or dried dill if you have none fresh. Whole tiny fingerling cucumbers and larger ones cut into chunks will swim deliciously in the brine as will any other firm-fleshed vegetables, such as onions, peppers and string beans. Try tossing in raw baby carrots, young peas in the pod, and cauliflower florets. Since the crock is an on-going process, you will have pickled vegetables in varying stages, from the mild, barely flavored ones to the zesty, full-flavored ones. Let your taste judge when they are ready. A few grape leaves or a sprig of cherry leaves added to the brine will help give a firmer pickle.

Since this is a long-brining process, be sure to check the crock each day and skim off any scum on the surface. In order to keep the vegetables below the brine, weigh down a dinner plate which covers the brine surface with a water-filled jar or freshly scrubbed rocks.

Should you like to preserve the last pickles left at the end of the garden season (if indeed there *are* any left!), let the pickles work in the crock 2 to 3 weeks, remove the pickles from the brine and pack into clean, hot jars. Strain and heat the brine, fill the jars to within 1/2 inch of the top, cap and process for 10 minutes.

Other Vegetables

Lots of other vegetables besides cucumbers lend themselves to pickling. In the bounty of the summer vegetable harvest, try these different ways to put up the surplus.

JERUSALEM ARTICHOKE PICKLES

8 quarts Jerusalem artichokes
  and vinegar to cover
2 cups salt
4 tablespoons turmeric
1 gallon vinegar
1 box mixed pickling spice, tied
  in a cloth bag

2 tablespoons turmeric
6 cups honey
small whole onions
medium red pepper pods

Wash the artichokes thoroughly and cut into bite-size chunks. Place in a large container and cover with vinegar. Add the salt and 4 tablespoons turmeric and let stand for 24 hours. Boil the gallon of vinegar, spice bag and 2 tablespoons turmeric for 20 minutes; then remove the spice bag, add the honey and bring the mixture to a boil again.

After the seasoning period, drain the artichokes and pack into sterilized jars. Pour the boiling syrup over the artichokes and add a red pepper pod and a small onion to each jar. Cap and process (see Table on page 10).

STRING BEAN PICKLES

1 peck green or wax beans
  (about 7-1/2 lbs.)
6 cups sugar
1-1/2 cups flour

scant 1/2 cup dry mustard
1 tablespoon turmeric
1 tablespoon celery seed
2 quarts vinegar

Prepare the beans as for the table. Cook slowly, with a bit of salt, until *just* tender. Do not overcook the beans because the hot pickling sauce will cook them more. Drain the beans thoroughly. Mix together the remaining ingredients and cook over *low heat* until thick. Stir almost constantly to prevent sticking. Pour the sauce over the cooked beans, fill sterilized jars with the mixture, and process (see Table on page 10) while hot.

SWEET-SOUR WAX BEANS

Serve this nearly forgotten delicacy with pork instead of applesauce.

2 lbs. wax beans, cut diagonally
  into 1-inch pieces
1 cup white vinegar
1/2 cup sugar
1 teaspoon celery seed

pinch of ginger
1 teaspoon dried summer
  savory (or 1 tablespoon
  chopped fresh)
small bay leaves

Cover the beans with water, add salt to taste and cook until just barely tender. Drain, saving the liquid; add to it the vinegar, sugar and spices. Add more water if needed so that there will be enough liquid to fill the packed jars. Bring the liquid to boiling, add the beans, bring to a boil again and pack the jars. Add a small bay leaf to each jar. Process (see Table on page 10). Makes about 4 pints.

DILLY BEANS

2 lbs. whole green beans
1 teaspoon cayenne pepper
4 cloves garlic
4 heads dill

2-1/2 cups water
2-1/2 cups white vinegar
1/4 cup salt

Pack the beans into hot sterilized pint jars lengthwise, leaving 1/4 inch headspace. To each jar add 1/4 teaspoon cayenne, 1 blanched garlic clove and 1 head dill. Combine the water, salt and vinegar; heat to boiling and pour while boiling over the beans, leaving 1/2 inch headspace. Cap and process. (See Table on page 10.) Makes 4 pints.

PICKLED BEETS

Boil 7 beets until tender, remove the skins, and slice lengthwise. Take equal parts of vinegar and sugar, 1 whole clove, a 1-inch cinnamon stick, and let boil. Place beets in a jar. Cover with the vinegar mixture. The beets will be ready to use in 3 days.

SWEET PICKLED CABBAGE

1 medium-size head cabbage
salt
1 pint vinegar
2/3 cup sugar

2 tablespoons mixed pickling
spice
4 4-inch pieces stick cinnamon

Cut the cabbage head into halves or quarters. After trimming away the finer outside leaves (keep them for slaw), boil the heart and stem part of the leaves in clear water and a little salt until quite tender. Drain well for 5 to 6 hours or overnight. Heat the vinegar, sugar and spices until boiling hot. Place the drained cabbage in a jar and pour the boiling hot vinegar mixture over it. When it is cold, it is ready to use and will keep about 2 weeks.

If you have a container large enough to accommodate the whole uncut cabbage, trim the outer leaves to within a couple of inches of the heart and pour the boiling syrup over the entire cooked cabbage. This whole pickled cabbage makes a very ornamental relish dish for a luncheon party or festival supper.

CARROT PICKLE

2 cups carrots
1 cup vinegar
1/2 cup sugar

1/4 cup water
1/2 tablespoon mixed pickling spice

Scrape the carrots and cut in thin strips lengthwise. Pack them in a pint jar. Boil the vinegar, sugar, water and spice in a glass or enamel saucepan for 10 minutes. Pour over the carrots. Process. (See Table on page 10.) This pickle may be used immediately, but is better after 6 weeks or more.

PICKLED EGGS

4 cups water
1 cup liquid from pickled beets
1 cup vinegar
2 tablespoons sugar
2 teaspoons mixed pickling spice
1/2 teaspoon salt

1 clove garlic
1 bay leaf
12 hard-cooked eggs, shelled
1 small onion, sliced and
separated into rings

In a large bowl or wide-mouth half-gallon jug, combine water, beet liquid and vinegar. Add sugar, pickling spice, salt, garlic clove and bay leaf and mix to dissolve sugar. Add the eggs and onion rings to the liquid. Cover and refrigerate about a week to season. Store these pickles in the refrigerator.

HOT DILL OKRA PICKLE

8 cups okra pods, 2-3 inches long
4 medium-size hot red peppers
2 cloves garlic, blanched
dill weed

2 cups vinegar
3/4 cup water
1/4 teaspoon turmeric
1/4 cup salt

Wash each okra pod well, leaving on about 1/4 inch of stem. Wash and stem the peppers. Pack okra, 1 pepper, a half clove garlic and a handful of dill weed into each of 4 sterilized pint jars. Bring to a boil the vinegar, water, turmeric and salt; reduce the heat. Pour the hot brine into the packed jars to within 1/2 inch of top. Place the uncapped jars in a pan of boiling water for 15 minutes, making sure the water cannot boil into the jars. Remove the jars, cap and seal. Best if seasoned at least 3 weeks before using and if served chilled.

PICKLED ONIONS

2 quarts small white onions
2 quarts white vinegar
12 whole cloves

1/2 teaspoon mace
1 teaspoon alum
1/2 tablespoon salt

Peel the onions and boil for 10 minutes in equal amounts of milk and water. Put the vinegar in a glass dish or porcelain pan. Add the cloves, mace, alum and salt. Scald well. Pack drained onions in sterilized jars and pour boiling liquid over them. Process. (See Table on page 10.) Keep at least 2 weeks before sampling.

DELMA'S PICKLED PEPPERS

6 red peppers
6 green peppers
6 yellow peppers
2-1/2 cups vinegar
1/2 cup sugar

2-1/2 cups water
2 teaspoons salt, divided
2 teaspoons mustard seed, divided
2 teaspoons whole allspice, divided

Remove tops and seeds from the peppers, cut in lengthwise quarters and set aside to drain. Combine the sugar, vinegar and water in a heavy saucepan and bring to a boil. Add the peppers and heat through. Remove the peppers from the syrup with a slotted spoon and pack them into hot, sterilized jars, adding to each jar 1/2 teaspoon salt, 1/2 teaspoon mustard seed and 1/2 teaspoon whole allspice. Cover with the hot vinegar mixture and process. (See Table on page 10.) Makes 4 pints.

SLICED GREEN TOMATO PICKLES

Green tomato pickles are excellent served with baked beans.

1 peck green tomatoes
1 cup salt
12 large onions
1 cup sugar
6 sweet red peppers, seeded

1 tablespoon ground allspice
1 tablespoon ground cinnamon
1 teaspoon ground cloves
1 tablespoon dry mustard
vinegar

Slice the tomatoes, sprinkle with the salt and leave overnight. In the morning drain off the liquid and slice the onions. Combine the tomatoes, onions, and all the other ingredients. Place in an open kettle, cover with cider vinegar, and boil until tender. Bottle and process. (See Table on page 10.) Makes about 6 quarts.

SWEET GREEN TOMATO PICKLE

1 peck green tomatoes
1 scant cup salt
1 cup vinegar
1 quart vinegar
3 lbs. light brown sugar (about 6-3/4 cups, packed)
3 tablespoons mixed pickling spice

3 red peppers, seeded and chopped
3 green peppers, seeded and chopped
1 tablespoon stick cinnamon
1 tablespoon whole cloves

Slice the tomatoes and sprinkle with the salt; let stand overnight. In the morning, drain them well and cook for a few minutes in small batches in the 1 cup vinegar. Make a thin syrup of the 1 quart vinegar, brown sugar, peppers and spices tied in a cloth bag. Cook the partially cooked tomatoes in this syrup until as done as you like them. Bottle and process. (See Table on page 10.)

MOTHER'S SLICED TOMATO PICKLE

1/2 peck green tomatoes
1 quart onions
1 cup salt
2 red peppers
4 sweet green peppers
vinegar
12 whole cloves

handful stick cinnamon
1 teaspoon allspice
3 cups brown sugar
3 tablespoons mustard seed
3 tablespoons celery seed

Slice the tomatoes and onions thin. Sprinkle with the salt and let stand overnight. In the morning, drain and rinse off the salt, remove the seeds from the peppers and chop the peppers fine. Put tomatoes, onions and peppers in a kettle and just cover with vinegar. Add a spice bag containing the cloves, cinnamon and allspice and cook until the vegetables are soft. Remove the spice bag; add sugar, mustard seed, celery seed and cook 10 minutes more. Process in jars. (See Table on page 10.)

TOMATO NASTURTIUM PICKLES

1 quart small ripe red and yellow tomatoes, mixed	salt
	vinegar
20 nasturtium pods	

Select blemish-free tomatoes and wash and wipe them dry. Pack the tomatoes into a sterilized jar, sprinkle with the nasturtium pods and a pinch of salt. Fill the jar to within 1/2 inch of the top with vinegar and process. (See Table on page 10.) Store in a cool place for about 6 weeks to season. Increase this recipe by keeping the same proportions of tomatoes and nasturtium pods.

MOTHER'S MUSTARD PICKLE

When there is a little of this vegetable and a little of that, a common occurrence at the end of the gardening season, try this mixed vegetable pickle. Pretty, zesty and a good way to use assorted vegetables.

4 quarts water	1 small bunch celery, cut fine
2 cups salt	1/2 cup flour
1 quart sliced cucumbers	4 tablespoons dry mustard
2 quarts sliced green tomatoes, cut up	1 teaspoon turmeric
	1-1/2 cups brown sugar
1 quart small button onions	cold water
1 cauliflower, broken into small pieces	2 quarts vinegar
	whole cloves
4 green peppers, seeded and chopped	stick cinnamon
4 red peppers, seeded and chopped	

Make a brine of the water and salt. Heat, pour over the vegetables, and leave overnight. In the morning, heat and scald the vegetables well in the brine; drain. Mix the flour, mustard, turmeric and brown sugar with enough cold water to make a smooth paste. Heat the vinegar, add the flour mixture, and cook, stirring, until smooth. Then add the vegetables, a few whole cloves and a couple of sticks of cinnamon. Allow to scald thoroughly, bottle and process (see Table on page 10).

Zucchini

Zucchini is as versatile as it is prolific (which is really saying something!) and makes excellent pickles, hard to distinguish from cucumbers. If the pickles are to be made in chunks, large zucchini may be used; for sliced or whole pickles, small, slender ones, 4 to 6 inches long are best.

BREAD AND BUTTER STYLE ZUCCHINI PICKLES

4 quarts zucchini, chunks or small slices
6 white onions, sliced
2 green peppers, seeded and chopped
2 red peppers, seeded and chopped
2 garlic cloves
1/2 cup salt
cracked ice

Put the vegetables, salt and garlic in a crock. Cover with cracked ice and let stand 3 hours. Drain, but do not wash. Make a syrup of 5 cups sugar, 3 cups cider vinegar, 1-1/2 teaspoons turmeric, 2 tablespoons mustard seed and 1 teaspoon celery seed. Bring the syrup to a boil and add the drained vegetables. Cook about 20 minutes; pack to within 1/2 inch of top of sterilized jars and process. (See Table on page 10.)

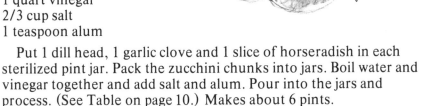

ZUCCHINI DILLS

6 heads of dill
6 garlic cloves
6 thin slices horseradish root
5 lbs. zucchini chunks
2 quarts water
1 quart vinegar
2/3 cup salt
1 teaspoon alum

Put 1 dill head, 1 garlic clove and 1 slice of horseradish in each sterilized pint jar. Pack the zucchini chunks into jars. Boil water and vinegar together and add salt and alum. Pour into the jars and process. (See Table on page 10.) Makes about 6 pints.

ZUCCHINI PICKLE

2 quarts thinly sliced, unpeeled
   zucchini
2 medium onions, thinly sliced
1/4 cup salt
2 cups vinegar

2 cups sugar
1 teaspoon celery seed
2 teaspoons mustard seed
1 teaspoon turmeric

Combine the zucchini and onions, sprinkle with the salt, cover with cold water and let stand 2 hours. Drain, rinse with fresh water, then drain again. Combine the remaining ingredients in a large pot and bring to a boil; boil 2 minutes. Add the vegetables, remove from the heat and let stand 2 hours. Bring again to boiling and cook 5 minutes. Pack in sterilized jars and process. (See Table on page 10.) Makes 4 pints.

MOCK WATERMELON PICKLES

3 lbs. peeled zucchini
4 tablespoons alum
3 quarts water
ice cubes
8 cups sugar

4 cinnamon sticks
4 cups vinegar
4 teaspoons cloves
1-1/2 cups sugar, divided

Cut the peeled zucchini in chunks. Heat alum in the water but do not boil. Pour this over the zucchini; cover with ice cubes and let stand for 2 hours. Drain. Bring the syrup ingredients to a boil; pour over the drained zucchini and let stand overnight. Drain and reheat this syrup 3 mornings, adding an additional 1/2 cup sugar each time, and pouring the syrup back over the zucchini. Boil up, pack into sterilized jars and process (see Table on page 10) on the third day.

Sauerkraut

Sauerkraut is one of the most commonly known brined vegetables. When brined in a crock, storage space for the crock may be a problem, for the sauerkraut has to ferment from 10 to 12 days. By using the in-the-jar method, space can be saved, and the kraut may be made in smaller batches with just as good a result.

SAUERKRAUT

Use good, sound heads of mature cabbage. Use 1 pound of salt with 40 pounds of cabbage; 3-1/2 tablespoons with 5 pounds of cabbage. One pound of cabbage will fill 1 pint jar.

Wash the heads and remove any green outside leaves or any damaged leaves. Quarter each head and shred the cabbage to about the thickness of a dime. In a large container, mix thoroughly 5 lbs. of the cabbage and 3-1/2 tablespoons of salt with the hands. Let it stand a few minutes to wilt so that the strands are not excessively bruised or broken in packing. Then pack the cabbage gently into a crock or large jar with a wooden spoon. Repeat until the crock is nearly full of the salted cabbage. Cover with a cloth, a clean plate and a weight to seal out any air from the fermenting cabbage. The salt will draw the moisture from the cabbage to form the brine. During the curing process, kraut requires daily attention. Skim off any scum as it forms, and wash and scald the cloth often to keep it free from scum and mold. Fermentation will be complete in 10 to 12 days or when no bubbles rise to the surface when the container is tapped lightly on the side.

As soon as the kraut is thoroughly cured, pack it into sterilized jars, tamping with the wooden spoon to remove air spaces, and filling jars to within 1/2 inch of the top with the brine from the crock or a brine made by dissolving 2 tablespoons salt in 1 quart of water. Cap and process (see page 10) in a boiling water bath.

SAUERKRAUT IN THE JAR

Prepare the cabbage as directed above. The amount of cabbage to be used may be altered as long as the 5 lbs. (2-1/2 quarts) of cabbage to 3-1/2 tablespoons of salt ratio is observed.

Pack the salted cabbage into sterilized jars, pressing it down firmly with a wooden spoon. The brine will form during fermentation and cover the cabbage.

Cover the packed cabbage with a pad of clean cheesecloth and insert two wooden strips crosswise so they catch under the neck of the jar (use tongue depressors or popsicle sticks). Set the packed jars in a shallow pan or on folded newspapers to catch any brine that might overflow. Screw on lids loosely and store in a dark place where the temperature is a fairly constant 70°F.

After about 10 days, if the temperature has been constant and directions for preparation were followed carefully, the brine level will drop suddenly. This means that the fermentation is almost complete.

Remove the cheesecloth and wooden strips and fill the jars to within 1 inch of the top with brine made by adding 1 tablespoon of salt to 1 quart of water. Press the cabbage down firmly to release gas bubbles. Cap and process in a boiling water bath. (See Table on page 10.)

Fruit Pickles

Fruits make delightful pickles that can add a special touch of color and flavor to the simplest soup-and-sandwich meal. And spicy pickled fruits are a wonderful garnish for meats.

MAPLE SWEET PICKLES

3 lbs. maple sugar
1 tablespoon cinnamon
1 teaspoon cloves

1 pint maple vinegar or cider
   vinegar
1 teaspoon allspice

Mix the above ingredients thoroughly with 7 lbs. plums, pears or peaches which have been halved or quartered and boil until the fruit is tender. Pack the fruit into jars with a slotted spoon, pour the hot syrup in the jar to within 1/2 inch of the top, cap and process. (See Table on page 10.)

SPICED FIGS

24 green or purple figs
4 cups cider vinegar
7 cups brown sugar, firmly packed

1 teaspoon grated lemon rind
2 2-inch sticks cinnamon
8-10 whole cloves

Select firm, barely ripe figs. Wash and drain. Combine the remaining ingredients in a large saucepan. Bring rapidly to boiling, stirring constantly until the sugar is dissolved. Reduce the heat; cook slowly, keeping the syrup boiling gently for 15 minutes. Add the figs; cook 2 minutes more. Cover and let stand at room temperature overnight. Spoon the figs into sterile jars. Heat the syrup to a full rolling boil and strain. Pour over the figs at once, cap and process. (See Table on page 10.) Store at least 1 week before using. Makes about 5 pints.

HEPZIBAH'S FRUIT PICKLE

A chopped fruit and vegetable pickle of sparkling color, mild and a bit spicy.

10 peaches, peeled and stoned
6 pears, pared and cored
4 large onions
30 ripe tomatoes
1 bunch celery
3 sweet red peppers, seeded
2 sweet green peppers, seeded

2 hot peppers, seeded
5 cups sugar
2 tablespoons salt
3 tablespoons mixed pickling spice
1 pint vinegar

Cut into chunks all the fruits and vegetables except the hot peppers; mix all together including the hot peppers; add the sugar, salt and vinegar and the pickling spice tied in a cheesecloth bag. Cook until thick, about 2 hours. Remove the hot peppers and spice bag before filling the jars. Using a slotted spoon, fill jars with the pickle, pour the hot syrup in to within 1/2 inch of the top and process. (See Table on page 10.)

DRIED FRUIT PICKLE

1 cup dried prunes
1 cup dried apricots
2 cups water
1-1/2 cups sugar
3/4 cup vinegar

12 whole cloves
1 teaspoon mustard seed
2 2-inch sticks cinnamon
1 teaspoon celery seed

Wash the fruit, cover with cold water and soak overnight. In the morning drain well and add 2 cups water. Simmer gently for 10 minutes. Add the remaining ingredients and cook slowly for about 1 to 2 hours, until the fruit is tender but holds its shape. Remove from the heat and let stand in the syrup until ready to use. When cool, store in the refrigerator in a covered jar.

SWEET PICKLED PEACHES

Use perfect, small peaches which will fit easily into wide-mouth pint jars.

8-10 firm ripe peaches
whole cloves
2 cups sugar

2 cups white vinegar
1 cup water
2 3-inch sticks cinnamon

Scald the peaches and pull off the skins. Leave whole (do not stone) and stick each with 3 cloves. Combine the sugar, vinegar, water, 6 cloves and cinnamon in an enamel kettle and boil covered for 5 minutes. Add the peaches a few at a time and continue boiling until peaches are soft, for about 15 or 20 minutes. Spoon peaches into hot sterilized jars and pour the syrup over the peaches, leaving 1/2 inch headspace. Process. (See Table on page 10.) Let stand a few weeks before using. Makes about 3 pints.

SPICED PEACHES

A darker pickle because of the brown sugar and cider vinegar. Peaches need not be perfect since they will be cut.

7 lbs. peaches, peeled and stoned	1 teaspoon whole cloves
4 lbs. dark brown sugar (about 9 cups)	1 teaspoon stick cinnamon
	1 teaspoon whole allspice
1 pint cider vinegar	1 teaspoon salt

Melt the sugar in the vinegar. Tie the spices in a cloth bag, put the bag and the salt in the syrup and bring the syrup to a boil. Put in the peaches and cook slowly until soft. Remove the peaches into a crock and pour the hot syrup over them. Cover the crock. Let stand overnight and for 6 successive days, drain the syrup from the crock, reheat it with the spice bag and pour it back over the peaches. Pickles may be left in the crock, or reheated with the syrup, packed into jars with the syrup poured in to within 1/2 inch and processed. (See Table on page 10.) Put whole cloves and cinnamon sticks in the filled jars before processing if desired.

SWEET PICKLED PEARS

Again, a darker pickle because of the sugar and vinegar.

4 quarts pears, pared and halved	4 4-inch sticks cinnamon
1 pint cider vinegar	whole cloves
2 lbs. brown sugar (about 4-1/2 cups)	

Boil the sugar, cinnamon and vinegar together for 20 minutes. Stick 2 cloves into each pear half and cook the pears in the syrup until soft. Place the pears in sterilized jars, strain the syrup, fill jars to within 1/2 inch of the top and process. (See Table on page 10.) Makes about 4 quarts.

GRANDMA RICKER'S SPICED PEARS

Lighter in color and a bit sweeter.

7 lbs. pears, pared and halved
8 cups sugar
1-1/2 pints white vinegar

stick cinnamon
whole cloves

Heat the sugar and vinegar to make a syrup and bring to a boil. For every quart of syrup, add 1 tablespoon each of stick cinnamon and whole cloves tied in a cloth bag and simmer the syrup and spices 15 minutes. Put in the pears and simmer for 30 minutes or until tender; do not cook soft. When the pears are easily pierced with a broomstraw, remove from the fire. Lift out the pear halves one by one with a slotted spoon and place in sterilized jars. Bring the syrup to a boil and pour over the pears, leaving 1/2 inch headspace. Process. (See Table on page 10.) Makes about 4 quarts.

PICKLED PINEAPPLE CHUNKS

1 No. 2-1/2 can pineapple chunks,
   drained
3/4 cup syrup from canned pineapple
3/4 cup vinegar

1-1/4 cups sugar
1/8 teaspoon salt
6-8 whole cloves
4-inch stick cinnamon

Heat together for 10 minutes all ingredients except the pineapple chunks. Add the drained pineapple and heat to boiling. Remove from the heat, pack with the syrup into sterilized jars and process (see Table on page 10), or store covered in the refrigerator. Makes 1 quart.

pear

pineapple

AUNT ANN'S WATERMELON PICKLE

Use the rind from your Fourth of July watermelon for this pickle.

rind of 1 large watermelon
2 quarts cold water
1/2 cup salt
2 tablespoons whole allspice
2 tablespoons whole cloves

10 2-inch pieces stick cinnamon
1 quart cider vinegar
1 quart water
8 cups sugar

Trim off the peel and all the pink part from the rind and discard. Weigh out 5 lbs. of prepared rind and cut into 1-inch pieces. Combine the 2 quarts water with the salt and soak the rind in this brine overnight. Drain and cover with fresh water and cook 1-1/2 hours or until almost tender. Add water as needed. Drain. Tie the spices in a cheesecloth bag and put this spice bag in a kettle with vinegar, the quart of water and sugar. Bring to a boil. Add the rind and boil gently for 2 hours. Remove the spice bag. Pack the rind in hot sterilized jars and fill with syrup to within 1/2 inch of the top. Process. (See Table on page 10.) Makes 6 pints.

PICKLED WALNUT MEATS

Unusual and very tasty served with game.

about 2 lbs. shelled walnut meats
1 pint vinegar

1 cup sugar
1 teaspoon cinnamon

Bring the sugar, vinegar and cinnamon to a boil. Add the walnut meats and simmer for 15 minutes. Pour the nut meats and syrup into jars, leaving 1/2 inch headspace and process. (See Table on page 10.) Makes about 2 pints.

2 Relishes

Relishes are chopped fruits or vegetables which are pickled with vinegar and sugar rather than by the long–brining process, although some relishes *are* brined for a few hours. (As for all pickles, use *pickling* salt when making relishes.) Hot or mild, sweet or tart, these combinations of peppers, onions, tomatoes, beets, cabbage and other vegetables and fruits seasoned with herbs and spices will arouse the taste buds of even the most devoted meat-and-potato eater.

Most relishes which are to be stored are cooked; many made to be eaten in a short time are uncooked. When cooking a relish, stir frequently to prevent the mixture from sticking. Relish is usually the consistency of a slightly thickened, medium gravy.

To process, ladle the hot mixture into hot sterilized jars, leaving 1/4 inch headspace. Process in a boiling water bath for 10 minutes. (Process cold relish for 20 minutes.)

APPLE AND CRANBERRY RELISH

1 cup ground raw cranberries
1 cup chopped raw apple, unpared
1 cup sugar

Mix and let stand an hour or two before serving. Store in a covered jar in the refrigerator.

CAPE COD RELISH

1 lb. (4 cups) fresh cranberries
2 apples, pared and cored
2 oranges
1 lemon

2-1/2 cups sugar (or 1-1/4 cups sugar and 1-1/4 cups corn syrup or honey)

Wash the cranberries and apples and put through a food grinder. Quarter the oranges and lemon, peel and all, remove seeds, and put through chopper. Add sugar and blend. Place in a jar, cover closely and chill. This makes 1-1/2 quarts relish and will keep indefinitely.

AUNT MARY'S APPLE PEPPER RELISH

2 sweet red peppers
3 tart apples, peeled and cored
2-1/2 or 3 large sweet onions, peeled

1/3 cup lemon juice
1 tablespoon grated lemon rind
1 cup sugar (or 2/3 cup honey)
1 teaspoon salt

Clean the peppers and remove the membrane and seeds. Put the pepper, onions and apples through a food grinder. Add the lemon rind and juice and heat to the boiling point. Add the sugar and salt and boil, stirring occasionally, until thick and syrupy — about 20 minutes. Fill hot sterilized jars and process. (See page 32.) Makes about 1 pint of relish, nice with ham or beef.

KIDNEY BEAN RELISH

1 small onion
1 or 2 hard-boiled eggs
2 cups kidney beans, cooked and drained
3 stalks celery

1 tablespoon mayonnaise
1 teaspoon crushed dill seed
1 teaspoon curry powder
1/2 teaspoon salt

Chop the onion, celery and eggs together. Add the beans and mix in the mayonnaise, dill seed and seasonings. Keep in the refrigerator and serve cool.

BEET RELISH

4 lbs. beets, cooked and peeled
4 large onions
3 large green peppers, seeded
1 tablespoon whole cloves

1-1/2 cups sugar
1-1/2 cups vinegar
1/4 cup water
1 tablespoon salt

Grind the beets, onions and green peppers. Tie the cloves in a cloth bag. In a large saucepan, combine the sugar, vinegar, water, salt and spice bag. Bring to a boil and reduce the heat. Add the vegetables, cover and simmer 20 minutes, stirring several times. Remove the cloves, pour into sterilized jars and process. (See page 32.) Makes 6 pints.

RED RELISH

4 cups chopped beets
1 cup chopped onions
1 cup chopped red sweet peppers
4 cups chopped cabbage
1 tablespoon horseradish

1 cup sugar (use 2 cups for a
  sweeter relish)
3 cups vinegar
1 tablespoon salt

Wash and drain the beets. Cover with boiling water and boil for 15 minutes; drain. Peel the beets and onions, remove seeds from the peppers. Combine all the chopped vegetables and add the remaining ingredients. Boil the complete mixture for 10 minutes. Pour boiling hot into sterilized jars and process. (See page 32.)

UNCOOKED BEET AND CELERY WINTER RELISH

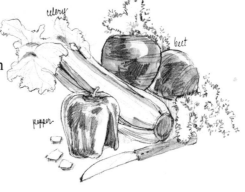

1-1/2 cups chopped cooked beets
1-1/2 cups celery, chopped medium
  fine
1/2 cup green pepper, chopped and
  seeded
2 teaspoons salt
1/3 cup horseradish
1/2 cup brown sugar
cold cider vinegar

Combine all the ingredients except the vinegar in the order given. Place the mixture in a 2-quart container, pour the vinegar over the mixture and cover closely. Let stand for at least 24 hours in the refrigerator for the flavors to blend.

CABBAGE RELISH

2 cups vinegar
3/4 cup sugar
1-1/2 teaspoons salt
1/4 teaspoon pepper

1/4 cup grated horseradish
2 cups chopped cooked carrots
2 cups chopped raw cabbage

Combine the vinegar, sugar, salt, pepper and horseradish; bring to the boiling point and boil 5 minutes. Add the vegetables and simmer 5 minutes longer. Put into sterilized jars and process (see page 32), or cool and use at once. Makes about 3 half-pint jars.

CABBAGE RELISH WITH CELERY

2 cups chopped raw cabbage
1 cup chopped celery
1 cup chopped carrots
2 cups vinegar

3/4 cup brown sugar
1-1/2 teaspoons salt
1/4 teaspoon pepper
1/4 cup grated horseradish

Prepare the vegetables. Combine the vinegar, sugar, salt, pepper and horseradish and boil 5 minutes. Add vegetables and simmer 10 minutes more. Process (see page 32) in sterilized jars or cool and use at once. Makes 3 half-pints of relish.

CALICO RELISH

2 cups celery, chopped
1/2 cup white onion, chopped
1 large red pepper
1 large green pepper

1/2 teaspoon salt
1 cup vinegar
1/4 cup sugar
1/2 teaspoon dry mustard

Chop the large stalks and tender leaves of celery and measure; prepare the onion. Remove seeds from the red and green peppers and chop fine. Cook the celery and onions in boiling water until tender; drain. Add the peppers, salt, vinegar, sugar and mustard. Simmer 10 to 15 minutes. Put into a sterilized jar and keep in the refrigerator for immediate use.

CARROT RELISH

8 large carrots, peeled
1 lemon
3/4 cup sugar

Put the carrots and whole lemon through a food grinder with a fine blade. Mix in the sugar and set the mixture in a jar in a cool place overnight. The relish is then ready to serve.

FRAN'S CHOW CHOW

1 gallon chopped green tomatoes
1 gallon chopped cabbage
1/2 gallon chopped onions
1 bunch celery
6 sweet peppers, seeded
6 hot peppers, seeded

3/4 cup salt
4 cups white sugar
1 lb. brown sugar (about 2-1/4 cups)
2 quarts cider vinegar
1 box pickling spice

Grind all the vegetable ingredients and sprinkle the salt over the mixture. Let this stand for 2 hours. Drain and put the vinegar, sugars and spice with the vegetables in a large kettle and cook for 1 hour. Pour the hot relish into sterilized jars and process. (See page 32.)

CHRISTMAS RELISH

12 cups coarsely ground zucchini squash
2 green peppers, coarsely ground and seeded
2 sweet red peppers, chopped and seeded
4 cups coarsely ground onions
1/3 cup salt

1 teaspoon turmeric
1 teaspoon curry powder
1 teaspoon celery seed
1 tablespoon cornstarch
1/2 teaspoon pepper
3 cups vinegar
4-1/2 cups sugar

In a large enamel pan, mix the salt with the vegetables. Let stand overnight. In the morning, drain off the salt water, rinse the vegetables with cold water and drain again. Mix together the rest of ingredients and add to the vegetables. Boil the mixture for 20 minutes. Pour into sterilized jars and process. (See page 32.)

CONFETTI RELISH

2 cups cabbage, shredded fine
3/4 cup green pepper, chopped very fine
1/2 cup sweet red pepper, chopped fine
2 cups raw carrot, grated

1 teaspoon celery seed
3 tablespoons brown sugar (or more to taste)
1/2 cup vinegar
1 teaspoon salt (or more to taste)
1/4 teaspoon dry mustard

Wash and prepare the vegetables; mix together. Add the remaining ingredients to the vegetable mixture and mix well. Let the relish stand 1 hour in a cold place and serve.

For a variation, substitute 3/4 cup celery (chopped fine, tops included) for the celery seed.

COPLEY PLAZA RELISH

1 quart green tomatoes, chopped
1/2 cup salt
1 quart ripe tomatoes, cut fine
5 small onions, chopped

3 red peppers, chopped
2 green peppers, chopped
1 pint vinegar
2 cups sugar

Cover the green tomatoes with the salt and let stand 12 hours. Drain the green tomatoes, add the other ingredients and cook the mixture for 30 minutes. Pour into sterilized jars and process. (See page 32.)

CORN RELISH

1 dozen ears sweet corn
2 onions, chopped
2 sweet green peppers, chopped
and seeded
1 sweet red pepper, chopped and
seeded

1 cup cabbage, chopped
2 tablespoons salt
1/4 teaspoon pepper
1-1/2 tablespoons dry mustard
1 cup sugar
2 cups vinegar

Cut the corn from the cobs but do not scrape the ears. Mix together the corn, onions, peppers and cabbage and add the remaining ingredients. Cook slowly for 1 hour, stirring occasionally. Pour into sterilized jars and process. (See page 32.) Makes about 5 half-pint jars.

CORN GARDEN RELISH

6 ears sweet corn
6 green peppers, seeded
4 red peppers, seeded
2 quarts half-ripe tomatoes
2 cups cucumbers
4 large onions

2 cups sugar
1 pint vinegar
2 tablespoons salt
2 teaspoons dry mustard
1 teaspoon turmeric

Cut the corn from the cobs, scraping the ears. Chop all the other vegetables. Mix corn with the chopped vegetables. Add the remaining ingredients and simmer the relish until fairly thick, stirring as needed. Put into sterilized jars and process. (See page 32.)

CRANBERRY RELISH

1 lb. (4 cups) cranberries
1 lemon

1 can crushed pineapple, drained
2 cups sugar

Grind the cranberries and lemon together; add the pineapple and sugar. Let the mixture blend and chill in the refrigerator for a few hours before serving. One cup of broken nutmeats may be added if desired.

SPICED CRANBERRY RELISH

2-1/2 cups sugar
1/2 cup water
2 2-inch sticks cinnamon
1 teaspoon whole cloves

2 tablespoons lemon juice
grated rind of 1 lemon
1 lb. (4 cups) fresh cranberries

Combine the sugar, water, spices, lemon juice and rind and boil together 5 minutes. Add the cranberries and cook slowly, without stirring, until all the skins have burst. Process (see page 32) in sterilized jars or chill for immediate serving. Makes 1 quart.

PRUNE AND CRANBERRY RELISH

1 lb. dried prunes, pitted
1 medium-size orange
1 cup water
1 cup sugar

2 cups cranberries
1 teaspoon lemon juice
1/8 teaspoon salt
1/3 cup chopped almonds

Peel the orange and remove the white membrane. Chop the orange pulp together with the orange rind and the prunes. Combine the water and sugar and bring to boiling, stirring until the sugar is dissolved. Boil for 5 minutes. Add the cranberries and simmer for 5 minutes, or until most of the skins have burst. Stir in the prune mixture, lemon juice, salt and almonds. Bring rapidly to boiling. Pour into sterilized jars and process. (See page 32.) Makes 2 quarts.

RAW CUCUMBER RELISH

1 large cucumber
1 teaspoon onion, minced
3/4 cup celery, sliced
1 tablespoon lemon juice

1/2 teaspoon salt
1/4 teaspoon paprika
dash of cayenne

Pare and seed the cucumber and chop fine; add the onion and celery. Blend together the lemon juice, salt, paprika and cayenne and add to the vegetables. Best if used at once, or will keep a few days in the refrigerator in a covered jar.

WINY FRUIT RELISH

A novel complement to pork, ham or game.

1 15-ounce box mixed dried fruit
1 cup sugar
1-1/2 cups dry white wine
1/2 cup brandy
1 3-inch stick cinnamon
2 lemon slices

Put the dried fruit into a 2-quart glass dish. Put the remaining ingredients into a saucepan and boil, stirring until the sugar dissolves. Pour the syrup over the fruit and mix well. Cover the dish and let stand for 3 days before using.

GARDEN RELISH

2 tablespoons butter
3 medium-size onions, chopped
3 large red peppers, chopped and
  seeded
2 medium-size tomatoes, peeled
  and sliced
1/2 teaspoon salt
1/8 teaspoon pepper

Melt the butter and sauté the onion in it for about 5 minutes or until a delicate golden color. Add the peppers, tomatoes, salt and pepper. Simmer the mixture for 30 minutes, stirring occasionally to prevent sticking. Put into a sterilized pint jar and process. (See page 32.)

HARVEST RELISH

4 cups ripe cucumbers
1 quart ripe tomatoes
2 cups onions
3 cups sugar
3 cups vinegar
1 tablespoon prepared mustard
2-1/2 tablespoons flour
1 teaspoon turmeric
salt and pepper to taste

Peel the cucumbers and tomatoes; cut these and the onions into fine pieces. Boil the vegetables and sugar together in the vinegar until the vegetables are tender. Make a paste of the mustard, flour and turmeric and add this mixture to the vegetables. Cook slowly until thickened, stirring as needed. Add the salt and pepper before putting the relish into sterilized jars. Process. (See page 32.)

HORSERADISH RELISH

1 cup grated horseradish roots
1/2 cup white vinegar
1/4 teaspoon salt

If you use whole horseradish, trim off the brown outer skin and wash before grating. Mix the grated horseradish, vinegar and salt thoroughly. Pack the mixture into sterilized jars. This relish keeps best if stored in the refrigerator.

HOT DOG RELISH

6 medium-size green tomatoes
2 large onions, peeled
1/2 head cabbage, cored
6 green peppers, seeded
1/4 cup salt
3 cups vinegar
3 cups sugar
1 cup water
1 tablespoon each mustard seed
    and celery seed
1 teaspoon turmeric
3 sweet red peppers, seeded and
    chopped fine

food grinder

Put the tomatoes, onions, cabbage and green peppers through the coarse blade of a food grinder. Mix with the salt, let stand overnight, then rinse and drain well. Boil the vinegar, sugar, water and spices together for 5 minutes, add all the vegetables and simmer for 10 minutes. Seal in sterilized jars and process. (See page 32.) Makes 4 pints.

MOTHER CUTTER'S RELISH

24 medium green tomatoes (or 30 small)   6 medium onions
2 stalks celery   2 rounded teaspoons salt
2 sweet green peppers, seeded   3 cups sugar
2 hot red peppers, seeded   3 cups vinegar

Put the vegetables through a food grinder. Sprinkle the chopped mixture with the salt and let stand 1 hour. Drain, add the rest of the ingredients and boil slowly for 1 hour, stirring occasionally. Process (see page 32) while hot.

MUSHROOM AND ARTICHOKE RELISH

1 cup button mushrooms or large   2 cups Jerusalem artichokes,
    mushrooms, quartered   peeled and diced
1-1/2 cups 1-inch lengths celery   1/2 cup lemon juice
                                   1 teaspoon sugar

Steam the mushrooms and celery for 5 minutes. Remove to a bowl. Steam the artichokes until barely tender, about 12 minutes. Add to the mushrooms and celery. Stir in the remaining ingredients and add enough water to cover the vegetables. Store in a covered jar in the refrigerator. This relish will keep a week or more.

ONION RELISH

2 cups chopped sweet Spanish onions
1/2 green pepper, seeded and diced
3 tablespoons diced pimiento
1/2 cup vinegar
1/4 cup water
1/4 cup sugar
2 teaspoons caraway seed
1/2 teaspoon salt

Combine the onions, green pepper and pimiento. Combine the vinegar, water, sugar, caraway seed and salt; bring to a boil and simmer 5 minutes. Pour over the onion mixture and refrigerate for several hours before serving.

BARTLETT PEAR RELISH

6 Bartlett pears, pared and cored
6 freestone peaches, peeled and stoned
6 ripe tomatoes, peeled
6 medium onions
3 green peppers, seeded
3 red peppers, seeded
5 cups sugar
1 quart cider vinegar
2 teaspoons salt
1 tablespoon mixed pickling spice tied in a bag
1 3-inch stick cinnamon

Chop the fruit and the vegetables fine. Mix with the remaining ingredients and boil together to a good relish consistency. Fill sterilized jars with relish and process. (See page 32.)

PEPPER-ONION RELISH

24 sweet peppers
2 hot peppers
18 large onions
3 cups sugar
3 tablespoons salt
1 quart vinegar

Seed the peppers and chop with the onions. Pour vinegar over the vegetables, sugar and salt. Boil 30 minutes, put into sterilized jars and process. (See page 32.)

SWEET PEPPER RELISH

12 red peppers, seeded
12 green peppers, seeded
3 medium-size onions
3 teaspoons salt
2 cups sugar (or more to taste)
1 quart vinegar

Grind the peppers and onions together in a food grinder with the medium blade. Cover with boiling water and let stand 10 minutes, then drain. Cover with fresh water and bring to a boil. Remove from the heat, let stand 10 minutes, then drain off the cooking liquid. Add the other ingredients and simmer for 15 minutes. Fill sterilized jars with relish and process. (See page 32.) Makes 5 pints.

OLD-FASHIONED HOT PEPPER RELISH

12 hot red peppers, seeded
12 hot green peppers, seeded
12 yellow onions
2 cups cider vinegar
3 tablespoons salt
2 cups sugar

Grind the peppers and onions, pour boiling water over them and let stand 5 minutes. Drain. Combine the remaining ingredients and bring to a boil. Add this syrup to the drained vegetables and boil for 5 minutes. Process (see page 32) the relish in sterilized jars.

GRANDMOTHER'S RED PEPPER RELISH

24 sweet red peppers, seeded (8 cups)
7 medium-size onions
3 cups vinegar
3 cups sugar
2 tablespoons salt

Cut the peppers and onions in half lengthwise and grind them, reserving the juices. In a saucepan combine the vegetable juice and vegetables, vinegar, sugar and salt. Simmer for 30 minutes, then process (see page 32) in sterilized jars. Makes about 5 pints.

MOTHER'S PICCALILLI

2 quarts green tomatoes
2 quarts ripe tomatoes, peeled
3 onions
3 ripe red peppers, seeded
3 green peppers, seeded
1 large cucumber
2 bunches celery
2/3 cup coarse pickling salt
3 pints vinegar
2 lbs. brown sugar (about 4-1/2 cups)
1 teaspoon dry mustard
1 teaspoon pepper

Chop all the vegetables and sprinkle with salt. Let stand at least 12 hours. Rinse and drain well and add the remaining ingredients. Cook slowly for 1 hour, stirring as needed, put into jars and process. (See page 32.)

UNCOOKED SAUERKRAUT RELISH

2 1-lb. cans sauerkraut
2 whole pimiento peppers, chopped
1/2 cup chopped green pepper
1 onion, diced
1-1/2 cups chopped celery
1/3 cup tomato catsup
1/4 cup vinegar
1/2 cup vegetable oil

Drain the sauerkraut in a sieve, pour hot water over it and drain again. Make a sauce of the catsup, vinegar and oil. Mix the sauerkraut with the other vegetables and pour the sauce over the mixture. Stir together and chill, covered, for several hours before serving.

UNCOOKED RELISH

4 cups chopped tomatoes
2/3 cup grated horseradish
   or 1/2 cup prepared horseradish
1 cup chopped onions
2 cups chopped celery
2 red peppers, seeded and chopped
2 green peppers, seeded and
   chopped

1/4 cup salt
1/4 cup mustard seed
1/2 teaspoon ground cinnamon
1/2 teaspoon ground cloves
1/2 teaspoon ground ginger
1/2 teaspoon ground mace
1 quart vinegar

Mix the chopped vegetables with the salt and spices. Pour the vinegar over all and mix well. Put into sterilized jars and process (see page 32) for 20 minutes.

ZUCCHINI RELISH

4 stalks celery, chopped
10 cups zucchini, peeled and
   chopped
4 large onions, chopped
1 red pepper, seeded and chopped
1/2 cup salt
3 cups vinegar
3-1/4 cups sugar
2-1/2 teaspoons celery seed
2-1/2 teaspoons mustard seed
2 teaspoons turmeric
2 tablespoons cornstarch,
   dissolved in 1/2 cup vinegar

Combine the vegetables and salt in a large enamel or stainless steel pan and let stand overnight. Next morning drain and rinse well. Combine and bring to a boil the 3 cups vinegar, sugar and seasonings. Add the chopped vegetables; remove from the heat and let stand for 2 hours. Return to the heat and bring to a boil. Add the cornstarch dissolved in vinegar and simmer 15 minutes. Spoon into sterilized jars and process in a boiling water bath for 20 minutes. Makes 15 half-pints.

3 Chutneys, Sauces & Catsups

Chutneys are the preserves of the condiment world — chopped fruits and vegetables combined with raisins and spices in a thick sweet-sour syrup. Rich brown chutney goes well with a whole range of meats and vegetables as well as the traditional curries and rice.

Catsups are a sort of condiment jam — and tomato is just one of the many you can concoct in your own kitchen. Use elderberries, grapes, lemons, mushrooms, plums and even walnuts to make delicious old-fashioned treats undreamed of by the fast-food chains and add a brand new zest to your condiment tray.

And instead of the ubiquitous Worcestershire or A-1, serve your own bottled sauces — made from celery, tomatoes, chili or *nasturtiums!*

As with the other condiments, the chutneys, sauces and catsups should be packed while hot into hot sterilized jars, leaving 1/4 inch headspace. Process chutneys and sauces in the boiling water bath for 10 minutes. Mushroom catsups should be processed for 30 minutes; process all other catsups for 5 minutes.

Chutneys

APPLE AND ONION CHUTNEY

3 lbs. cooking apples
2 lbs. onions
1 lb. light brown sugar (about 2-1/4 cups)
1 tablespoon salt

1 tablespoon ground ginger
2 tablespoons mustard seed
1/2 lb. light seedless raisins
1 pint vinegar
3/4 teaspoon pepper

Chop the apples and onions into fine bits and mix with the other ingredients. Boil the mixture in a kettle for 45 minutes, stirring as needed to prevent scorching. Bottle and process. (See page 44.)

GINGER CHUTNEY

15 large tart apples
4 sweet green peppers
1 small chili pepper
2 onions
1 cup preserved ginger, with syrup
1 cup seedless raisins
3 cups vinegar
1 cup water

1/4 teaspoon whole cloves
1 small bay leaf
2 tablespoons white mustard seed
1 teaspoon whole allspice
1-1/2 cups brown sugar
1/2 tablespoon salt
1 teaspoon ground ginger

Pare, core and chop the apples. Seed the peppers and chop up together with the onions. Mince the preserved ginger. Mix all these with the raisins, vinegar and water in a heavy enameled or stainless steel kettle. Add the whole spices tied in a bag and simmer gently for 2 hours. Add the sugar, salt and ground ginger and boil down to a thick mixture. Remove the spice bag before bottling. Process. (See page 44.) Makes about 6 pints.

TANGY CRANBERRY APPLE CHUTNEY

12 sour apples
1 cup seedless raisins, chopped
1 pint cider vinegar
1 pint chopped cranberries
2 cups sugar

juice of 4 lemons
1 red pepper, minced and seeded
2 green apples, minced
1/2 teaspoon cayenne pepper
1 tablespoon ground ginger

Pare, core and chop the sour apples. Put into a kettle and add the remaining ingredients. Stir together and simmer the mixture until thick. Pack in sterilized jars and process. (See page 44.) Makes about 4 pints.

CRANBERRY CHUTNEY

4 cups cranberries
2 cups sugar
1 cup water
1/4 teaspoon baking powder

1/2 teaspoon salt
1 cup seedless raisins
1 cup thick orange peel, slivered

Place all the ingredients except the raisins and orange peel in a large kettle and stir to mix. Cover tightly and boil slowly for 15 minutes. Remove from the heat and cool with the cover still on the kettle. If the cover remains in place until the cranberry mixture is cold, the berries will remain whole.

Stir the raisins into 1 cup hot water and boil 5 minutes until plump. Drain the fruit and cool. Boil the orange peel in 1 cup hot water for 5 minutes; drain and cool. Combine the cranberry mixture, raisins and orange peel, mixing carefully so that the berries are not crushed. Pack into sterilized jars and process (see page 44) or store in the refrigerator. Makes about 3 pints.

PEACH-APPLE-ONION CHUTNEY

3 lbs. peaches
4 lbs. apples
3 lbs. onions
1 lb. seedless raisins

1/4 lb. ginger root
1 teaspoon salt
2 cups vinegar
4 cups sugar

Peel and stone the peaches. Peel and core the apples. Peel the onions. Chop all these ingredients fine. Mince the raisins and ginger root and add to the fruits and onions. Mix all with the salt, vinegar and sugar. Boil 1 hour, stirring to prevent scorching. Bottle and process. (See page 44.)

VICKY CRAN'S PEACH CHUTNEY

1/2 cup chopped onion
1/2 lb. seedless raisins
1 small clove garlic, peeled
4 lbs. fresh peaches
2 tablespoons red chili powder
2/3 cup chopped crystallized ginger

2 tablespoons mustard seed
1 tablespoon salt
1 quart vinegar
1-1/2 lbs. brown sugar (about 3-3/8 cups)

Put the onions, raisins and garlic through a food grinder, using the fine blade. Peel the peaches, cut into small pieces and mix with the other ingredients. Stirring occasionally to prevent scorching, boil the mixture slowly for an hour or more or until the chutney is a rich brown color and rather thick. Bottle and process. (See page 44.) Makes about 3 pints.

ROSY CHUTNEY

1-1/2 cups seedless raisins
3 cups diced apples
1 cup chopped onions
1 cup vinegar
1 cup sugar

1 6-oz. can tomato paste
3/4 cup water
1/2 teaspoon salt
1/4 teaspoon each of cayenne,
black pepper and ginger

Rinse and dry the raisins, place in a heavy saucepan and add the remaining ingredients. Boil the mixture slowly for about 1 hour. Bottle and process. (See page 44.) Makes 1 quart.

TOMATO-APPLE CHUTNEY

2-1/2 quarts ripe tomatoes,
peeled, cored and chopped
1 quart apples, pared, cored and
chopped
2 cups chopped cucumber
1-1/2 cups chopped onions
1-1/2 cups chopped sweet red
peppers, seeded

1 cup seedless raisins
3 cups brown sugar, firmly packed
3 cups vinegar
1 hot red pepper
1 clove garlic, peeled and crushed
1 tablespoon ground ginger
1 teaspoon salt
1 teaspoon ground cinnamon

Combine all the ingredients in a large kettle and cook slowly until thick, about 2 hours. Stir often to prevent sticking and scorching. Pour the hot mixture into sterilized jars, cap and process. (See page 44.) Makes 3 pints.

Sauces

CELERY SAUCE

15 small ripe tomatoes
1 small green pepper, seeded
1-1/2 tablespoons salt
2 large bunches celery

1 scant cup sugar
2 cups vinegar
2 onions

Chop all the vegetables and mix with the other ingredients. Boil until thick. Bottle and process. (See page 44.)

SHAKER CHILI SAUCE

48 ripe tomatoes
10 peppers, seeded
2 large onions
2 quarts vinegar
4 tablespoons salt

2 teaspoons each of ground cloves,
  cinnamon, nutmeg and allspice
1 cup sugar
1 teaspoon each of mustard and
  curry powder (optional)

Slice the tomatoes and chop the peppers and onions together. Add the vinegar and spices and boil until thick. Process in sterilized jars. (See page 44.)

WINSLOW CHILI SAUCE

24 ripe tomatoes
3 good-size onions
3 green peppers or 1 hot and 2
  sweet peppers
1 quart cider vinegar
1 cup sugar
1 tablespoon salt
1 whole nutmeg, grated
1 teaspoon ground allspice
1 teaspoon ground cinnamon
1 teaspoon ground cloves

Scald the tomatoes and remove the skins and blossom ends. Seed the peppers and chop coarsely. Chop the onions fine. Stir all the ingredients together in a large kettle and cook for 1 hour. Let the mixture stand overnight. In the morning, stir and bring to boiling. Put into sterilized jars and process. (See page 44.)

DEANNA'S NASTURTIUM SAUCE

1 quart nasturtium flowers
1 quart vinegar
8 shallots, well bruised
6 whole cloves

1 teaspoon salt
1/2 teaspoon cayenne pepper
1/2 teaspoon soy sauce

Simmer together the vinegar, shallots, cloves, salt and pepper for 10 minutes. Add the soy sauce and pour the mixture over the flowers. Cover tightly and let stand for 2 months. Strain and pour into bottles and process. (See page 44.)

Catsups

ELDERBERRY CATSUP

A perfect condiment for game of all kinds.

2 quarts elderberries
vinegar
1 cup sugar
1 teaspoon ground cinnamon

1 tablespoon ground allspice
1 tablespoon ground cloves
1/4 teaspoon cayenne pepper

Put the elderberries in a saucepan and cover with vinegar. Cook at medium heat until the berries burst. Put them through a sieve, and add the sugar and spices to the pulp. Simmer the mixture until thick. Pour into sterilized jars and process. (See page 44.)

SPICED GRAPE CATSUP

Goes well with chicken, lamb or pork.

5 lbs. grapes
3 lbs. brown sugar (about 6-3/4 cups)
2 teaspoons ground cinnamon

2 teaspoons ground allspice
1/2 teaspoon ground cloves
1/4 cup vinegar

Peel the grapes, reserving both pulp and skins. Boil the skins until tender. In a separate pan, cook the pulp until it rubs easily through a colander. Add the sieved pulp to the cooked skins along with the sugar, spices and vinegar. Boil the mixture until thick, taking care to stir often, for sticking can be a problem. Bottle and process. (See page 44.)

MRS. RUSSELL'S LEMON CATSUP

15 large lemons
1-1/4 lbs. salt
1 teaspoon each of ground mace, nutmeg, cayenne pepper and allspice

1 gallon vinegar
8 or 9 cloves garlic
1/4 lb. dry mustard

Slice and seed the lemons. Add the other ingredients and simmer 20 to 30 minutes. Put the mixture in a jar and cover it. Stir it well every day for 7 or 8 weeks. Strain, bottle and process. (See page 44.)

Mushroom catsup is a time-tested, but hard-to-find, concoction that gives a wonderful flavor to sauces, gravies and stews. Here are two variations.

MUSHROOM CATSUP

2 lbs. fresh mushrooms
2 tablespoons salt
1 bay leaf
1/4 cup cider vinegar
4 whole cloves

1 4-inch stick cinnamon
1/2 teaspoon whole allspice
4 strips fresh lemon peel
1/4 cup brandy

Wipe the mushrooms clean and break into pieces; layer the mushrooms in a large bowl with the salt. Bury the bay leaf in the center of the salted mushrooms and let the mixture stand for 24 hours, turning the mushrooms over 3 or 4 times. Tie spices and lemon peel into a bag, bring to a boil in the vinegar and simmer for 15 minutes; cool. Put the mushrooms through the coarse blade of a food grinder. Remove the spice bag from the vinegar and combine the mushrooms and their liquid with the vinegar. Simmer for 30 minutes. Purée the cooked mixture in a blender, a small amount at a time, adding the brandy gradually. Pour into sterilized jars, seal and process in water bath for 30 minutes. Makes 3 six-ounce jars.

GRANDMOTHER AHREND'S MUSHROOM CATSUP

10 lbs. fresh mushrooms
1/2 cup salt
1 small onion, chopped
dash cayenne pepper

1 teaspoon ground allspice
1 teaspoon ground cloves
1 teaspoon horseradish
1 cup vinegar

Chop the mushrooms and mix with the salt. Let stand overnight. Mash this mixture and add to it the chopped onion, spices and vinegar. Boil in an enameled kettle until thick. If the mixture gets too thick, it may be thinned with vinegar. The mixture may be strained while hot, if desired. Pour into sterilized jars and process for 30 minutes. Makes about 5 pints.

PLUM CATSUP

Boil ripe plums, skins and all, with a little water, and, when soft, strain through a colander, pressing the pulp through. To each 5 lbs. of plum pulp and juice, add 3 lbs. light brown sugar (about 6-3/4 cups), 1 pint cider vinegar, 1/8 teaspoon black or cayenne pepper, 1 tablespoon each of salt, ground cinnamon and mace and 2 teaspoons ground cloves. Boil the mixture for 20 minutes, bottle and process. (See page 44.)

TOMATO CATSUP

half bushel ripe tomatoes
1/3 cup salt
1 tablespoon whole cloves, tied
   in a bag
1 whole nutmeg, grated

1 tablespoon ground mace
1/2 teaspoon cayenne pepper (or
   more to taste)
1 quart cider vinegar

Press the tomatoes through a sieve until all the pulp is out. Put the pulp into a porcelain or enamel kettle; when it begins to boil, add the other ingredients. Cook slowly, stirring occasionally to prevent sticking, for 1-1/2 hours. Remove the clove bag. Bottle while hot and process. (See page 44.)

WALNUT CATSUP

Husk and bruise to a mass 120 green walnuts gathered when a pin could prick the skin, reserving the husks. Add to the nuts 3/4 cup of salt and 4 cups good vinegar. Place in a crock and stir every day for a fortnight. After this time, strain and squeeze the liquor from the mixture and set aside.

Pour 1-1/2 cups vinegar over the nut husks and let stand overnight. Strain and squeeze as with the nut mixture. Put the two liquors together and add 1-1/8 ozs. peppercorns, 40 whole cloves, 3/4 oz. nutmeg, sliced, and 3/4 oz. ginger root. Boil closely covered for 3/4 hour and then strain, bottle and process (see page 44) in sterilized jars.

4 Mincemeats

The spicy, rich aroma of mince pie has long bolstered spirits on fall and winter holidays. Those who feel suet is for the birds can make mock or green tomato fillings for this traditional dessert — plenty of flavor minus the meat.

Use ground spices for mincemeat. Some prefer their mincemeat laced with brandy, sherry or rum; others feel that it is cider that gives the filling just the proper edge. The meat and fruits may be either chopped or ground, and the mixture should be cooked down to a thick, brown mass — *mincemeat,* that pungent combination of meat, fruit and spices.

The boiled cider called for in the Boiled Cider (p. 54), Seven-Day (p. 55), and Green Tomato with Boiled Cider (p. 58) Mincemeats is sweet cider which has been boiled down into a thick, rich, dark syrup. This syrup was traditionally made in the fall in copper kettles, great barrels of cider boiled down until about 7 gallons of syrup from each barrel of cider remained. When preparing boiled cider, the quantity of cider must be reduced by about eight times; that is, if your recipe calls for a pint of boiled cider, you must boil down a gallon of cider. Rather than heating all the cider at once, begin with a fourth of it and gradually add the remainder as the cider boils down.

All mincemeats should be stirred frequently during the long cooking time to prevent scorching. An asbestos pad placed between the pan and the heat source may also be helpful.

Mincemeat should be processed in a pressure canner to prevent spoilage of the meat in the mixture. Leave 1 inch headspace in the jars, process quarts for 25 minutes at 10 pounds of pressure and store the jars in a cool, dark, dry place. The green tomato mincemeats on p. 57 and p. 58, may be processed in a boiling water bath since they contain no meat or suet. Fill jars to within 1/2 inch of the top and process for 20 minutes.

MINCEMEAT

2 lbs. lean beef
1 lb. suet
4 lbs. apples
2 oranges
2 lbs. currants
1 lb. golden seedless raisins
2 lbs. dark seedless raisins
1/2 lb. citron
6 cups brown sugar

2 teaspoons ground nutmeg
1 tablespoon ground allspice
1 tablespoon ground cinnamon
1/4 teaspoon ground ginger
1 teaspoon ground cloves
1 tablespoon salt
4 tablespoons lemon juice
4 cups cider or grape juice

Cook the beef until done. Cool. Chop the beef and the suet. Wash, core, pare and chop the apples. Finely chop the peel of 1 orange and pulp of both oranges. Mix all of the ingredients and simmer for 1 hour. Pack hot into hot jars, processing pints and quarts for 25 minutes at 10 pounds pressure.

MINCEMEAT WITH SPIRITS

2 lbs. lean beef
1 lb. beef suet
5 lbs. apples
2 lbs. seedless raisins
2 lbs. currants, mashed
1 lb. golden seedless raisins
3/4 lb. citron, cut fine
2 tablespoons each of ground
  cinnamon and mace

1 tablespoon each of ground
  cloves and allspice
1 teaspoon ground nutmeg
1 tablespoon salt
2-1/2 lbs. brown sugar (about
  5-5/8 cups)
1 quart sherry
1 pint brandy

Boil the beef and when cold, chop fine. Mince the suet and peel, core and chop the apples. Mix these ingredients with the raisins, currants and citron. Add the spices, salt and sugar and mix well. When all is well mixed, stir in the sherry and brandy. Mix thoroughly and pack in a stone crock for several weeks before using so that it may ripen and mellow. After this time, pack into sterilized jars and process under pressure. (See page 10.)

HOLIDAY MINCEMEAT

3 lbs. lean beef, chopped fine
2 lbs. chopped suet
3-1/2 quarts apples, peeled and chopped fine
3 lbs. seedless raisins, chopped
2 lbs. currants
1-1/4 lbs. citron, cut in small pieces
1/2 cup chopped candied orange peel
1/2 cup chopped candied lemon peel
1/2 cup lemon juice
1/2 cup orange juice
2 tablespoons salt
4 cups sugar
1 cup black coffee
2 cups cider
1-1/4 teaspoons ground cloves
1 teaspoon ground allspice
2 teaspoons ground cinnamon
1 cup currant jelly
4 cups brandy
1/2 cup sherry

Mix all the ingredients except the sherry and the brandy and cook for about 2 hours. When cool, not cold, add the liquor and let stand in an earthenware crock for at least a week before using. Makes about 12 quarts and will keep an indefinite period of time in a cool place or may be packed in sterilized jars and processed. (See page 10.)

BOILED CIDER MINCEMEAT

Makes enough filling for 10 pies.

5 quarts apples, peeled and finely chopped
3 lbs. beef flank or chuck (with some fat on it)
1 quart meat broth
1 pint boiled cider (see page 52)
3 cups molasses
1 lb. seedless raisins
1/2 lb. seeded raisins
4 cups sugar
1 small jar candied orange peel
1 teaspoon pepper
5 teaspoons ground cinnamon
3 teaspoons ground cloves
1 teaspoon ground nutmeg
1 tablespoon salt

In an 8- or 10-quart kettle, cover the meat with hot water, salt lightly and cook 2 to 3 hours, or until the meat falls from the bones. Measure the broth and add water as needed to make the necessary quart. If the broth is more than 1 quart, boil it down, not pouring off the fat. After the meat has cooled, put it through the medium blade of a food grinder.

Put the chopped meat and broth back into the kettle and add the other ingredients, mixing all together thoroughly. Cook slowly on top of the stove or in a 350°F oven. Stir frequently if you are cooking on the stove, occasionally if you use the oven. Cook for 2 or 3 hours or until the apples are very soft, but be careful not to let all the liquid evaporate. This mincemeat will keep for many weeks in a cold place in unsealed jars or a crock; for gifts or for keeping indefinitely, fill sterilized jars with the mixture and process under pressure. (See page 10.)

This basic recipe may be varied according to supplies available. Dried currants may be used instead of raisins. Two tablespoons of grated orange peel and juice from any canned fruit, spiced peaches or pears, and bits of leftover jelly can be added. More than 5 quarts of apples may be put in and a little more or less meat will not spoil the brew.

UNCOOKED ENGLISH MINCEMEAT

1 lb. beef suet, chopped fine	1 teaspoon ground cinnamon
1-1/2 lbs. apples, pared, cored and chopped	1/2 teaspoon each ground nutmeg, cloves, ginger and allspice
1 lb. seedless raisins	
1 lb. dried currants	1 teaspoon salt
1 lb. sugar	2 teaspoons vanilla
1/4 lb. citron, chopped fine	1 small bottle maraschino cherries with juice
grated rind and juice of 2 oranges and 1 lemon	

Mix all the ingredients thoroughly and let stand for several hours. Mix again and pack into sterilized jars. No cooking is needed. Process under pressure (see page 10) if mincemeat is to be stored.

SEVEN-DAY MINCEMEAT

Enough filling for three large pies.

1/2 lb. beef, cooked and chopped	1/2 teaspoon ground cinnamon
1/2 teaspoon salt	1/2 whole nutmeg, grated
1/4 teaspoon pepper	1/2 lb. currants
1/2 lb. suet, chopped	2 lbs. raisins, seeded
chopped, cooked apples twice the bulk of the suet	1/2 lb. citron
	1/2 lb. orange peel
1/2 lb. brown sugar (about 1-1/8 cups)	1 glass grape jelly
	1 cup boiled cider (see page 52)
1/2 teaspoon ground mace	1/2 pint brandy
1/2 teaspoon ground cloves	1/4 pint sherry

Mix all the ingredients except the brandy and sherry and bring to a boil. Cool the mixture and add the brandy and sherry. Put in jars for 1 week. If you would like to store this, pack in sterilized jars and process. (See page 10.) When ready to use, add 1 tablespoon French brandy to each pie.

OLD-FASHIONED CIDER MINCEMEAT

6 lbs. beef cubes
1 lb. suet
2 lemons, quartered
9 lbs. apples, pared and cored
2 lbs. seedless raisins
2 lbs. currants
1 lb. citron
8 cups sugar

6 nutmegs, grated
1 tablespoon ground allspice
1 quart cider (sweet or hard,
　according to preference)
vinegar
ground cinnamon
ground cloves
salt

In a large kettle, simmer the beef cubes in water to cover until tender. Drain and grind the beef together with the suet, lemons and apples. Return to the kettle and add all the other ingredients. Cook until heated through, stirring constantly. Add vinegar, cinnamon, cloves, and salt to taste. While still at a low boil, put into sterilized jars and process. (See page 10.)

GREAT-GREAT GRAM'S MINCEMEAT

When you are making the pies, add brandy or rum to taste and a few drops of rose water. Sprinkle each pie with sugar and nutmeg. Dot with butter before putting top pie crust on. Press bottom and top crusts together with a moistened fork.

4 cups chopped beef
10 cups chopped apples
2 cups beef broth
2 cups sour cider
5 cups sugar
1 cup molasses
3 tablespoons ground cinnamon

2 teaspoons ground cloves
4 lemons, rind and juice
3 tablespoons salt
1 lb. seedless raisins
1/2 lb. citron
1/4 lb. orange rind
1/4 lb. lemon rind

Put the meat and apples through the coarse blade of a food grinder. Put this into a large kettle and add the other ingredients. Simmer slowly for 2 hours. To make the beef broth, simmer 3 lbs. of stew meat or middle cut of shin for 2 hours, adding only enough boiling water to leave about 2 cups beef liquid (or use 2 bouillon cubes). Pack hot into sterilized jars and process. (See page 10.)

MAMA FOOTIE'S MINCEMEAT

4 cups lean beef, chopped after
   slow boiling
3 lbs. seedless raisins
1 lb. currants
4 cups brown sugar
1 cup molasses
1 cup chopped suet

9 cups chopped apples
4 cups meat broth
6 teaspoons salt
8 teaspoons ground cinnamon
3 teaspoons each of ground
   cloves and mace
juice of 6 lemons

   Combine all the ingredients and simmer about 2 hours. Store in jars in a cool place if to be used in 2 weeks; if storing longer, pack into sterilized jars and process. (See page 10.)

MAPLE MINCEMEAT

4 cups chopped cooked beef
1 cup butter
1 cup chopped suet
2 cups seedless raisins
4 cups maple sugar
2 cups molasses

8 cups chopped apples
1 tablespoon ground allspice
1 tablespoon ground cloves
1 tablespoon ground cinnamon
8 cups sweet cider

   Mix thoroughly all the ingredients and boil slowly in sweet cider for 2 or 3 hours. Process under pressure (see page 10) in sterilized jars.

GREEN TOMATO MINCEMEAT

6 cups chopped apples
6 cups chopped green tomatoes
4 cups brown sugar
1-1/3 cups vinegar
3 cups seedless raisins
3 teaspoons ground cinnamon
1 teaspoon ground cloves
3/4 teaspoon ground allspice
3/4 teaspoon ground mace
3/4 teaspoon pepper
2 teaspoons salt
3/4 cup butter

   Mix the apples with the tomatoes and drain. Add remaining ingredients, except butter; bring gradually to the boiling point, and boil until thick, stirring occasionally. Add the butter and turn into sterilized jars. Process 20 minutes in a boiling water bath.

GREEN TOMATO MINCEMEAT WITH BOILED CIDER

8 quarts green tomatoes
3 lbs. brown sugar (about 6-3/4 cups)
1 cup vinegar
1 teaspoon salt
1 pint boiled cider (see page 52)

2 lbs. seeded raisins
1 tablespoon ground cloves
1 tablespoon ground cinnamon
1 tablespoon ground nutmeg
1 tablespoon ground allspice

Mix all the ingredients together in a kettle and simmer for 2-1/4 hours. Put into sterilized jars and process for 20 minutes in a boiling water bath.

MOCK MINCEMEAT

Enough for one pie.

1-1/3 cups sugar
1/2 teaspoon salt
1/2 teaspoon ground cinnamon
1/4 teaspoon ground cloves
1/4 teaspoon ground ginger
1-1/2 cups apple, pared and
   finely chopped
1 cup seedless raisins

1/2 cup canned jellied cranberry
   sauce, broken up
1/3 cup coarsely chopped walnuts
1 teaspoon grated orange peel
1/2 teaspoon grated lemon peel
1/4 cup lemon juice
butter

Mix together in a bowl the sugar, salt and spices. Add the remaining ingredients and mix well. Pour the filling into an unbaked pie shell, dot with butter and cover with a second crust. Prick holes in the crust to allow steam to escape. Bake the pie at 400°F for 30-35 minutes or until nicely browned. Serve warm with thin slices of sharp cheddar cheese.

5 Homemade Beverages & Syrups

Long before the cola and soda pop people made big business out of bottled drinks, families mixed and put up their own. Try these old-fashioned treats on *your* family. There is nothing quite as refreshing on a sweltering summer's day as an ice-cold glass of fruit shrub or a cool cup of gingery switchel. And your own homemade beer, spring tonic or dandelion wine adds an inimitable fillip to your hospitality.

Shrubs

To serve mix about one-quarter cup of shrub with water and ice in a tall glass. Adjust the shrub and water to your taste.

To store these, pour into sterilized bottles and cork or cap. To seal, dip the capped bottle in melted wax, allowing the wax to cover both cork or cap and the upper neck of the bottle.

BLACKBERRY SHRUB

Put 3 or 4 quarts fresh berries in an earthen crock. Add vinegar to cover the berries and cover the crock with a dinner plate. Let stand for 2 weeks. Strain out the berries, not pressing the pulp. To the liquid in the crock, add equal parts of honey, cup for cup. Stir until the honey is completely dissolved. Store in sterilized bottles.

RASPBERRY SHRUB

Mash 4 quarts of raspberries and cook gently until the seeds come loose from the pulp. Strain through cheesecloth as for jelly. For every cup of fruit juice, add 1/2 cup cider vinegar and 2 cups sugar. Put the mixture in a saucepan and heat, stirring until sugar dissolves. Boil until a thick syrup consistency is reached. Let stand a few minutes off the heat and skim if necessary. Strain, bottle and seal.

STRAWBERRY SHRUB

Pour 3 quarts of cider vinegar over 9 lbs. of ripe strawberries and let stand for 24 hours. Bring the mixture to a boil, strain, add sugar in the amount of 3 cups of sugar for every 2 cups juice. Boil the fruit juice with the sugar 5 minutes then strain again. Bottle and seal.

Switchels

These may be chilled, but switchel served in the hayfield was never served colder than the well water it was made from.

HAYMAKERS' SWITCHEL

1 gallon cool water
2 cups sugar
1 cup molasses

1 cup vinegar
1 teaspoon ground ginger

Mix all ingredients thoroughly. Good served chilled or just as is.

GINGER SWITCHEL

3/4 cup sugar or honey
4 tablespoons vinegar

1 teaspoon ground ginger
2 quarts cool water

Mix ingredients together thoroughly.

HAYFIELD CIDER

1/2 cup molasses
1 teaspoon ground ginger

1/2 cup boiled cider (see page 52)
2 quarts cool water

Stir the ingredients together thoroughly. The old recipe says, "Put in a stone jar and hang in the well to cool."

Assorted Beverages

APPLE NOG

1 egg
1 tablespoon sugar
1 cup chilled apple juice or cider
3/4 cup milk
fresh nutmeg

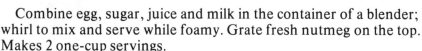

Combine egg, sugar, juice and milk in the container of a blender; whirl to mix and serve while foamy. Grate fresh nutmeg on the top. Makes 2 one-cup servings.

GINGER BEER

Mix 3 cups sugar with 3 ozs. strong white ginger and the grated peel of 2 lemons. Put these ingredients into a large stone jar and pour over them 2 gallons boiling water. When lukewarm, strain and add the juice of 2 lemons and 2 tablespoons of yeast. Let the mixture stand overnight and bottle in the morning.

ROOT BEER

To each gallon of water, add 1/2 ounce each of hops, burdock yellow dock, sarsaparilla, dandelion and spikenard. Boil about 20 minutes and strain while hot.

Add 8 to 10 drops of the oils of spruce and sassafras and cool to lukewarm. Add 2 tablespoons yeast and 2/3 pint molasses or 1 cup sugar. Cover the liquid with a cloth for 2 hours, bottle and store in a cool place.

SPRING BEER

1 handful wintergreen berries
3 sassafras roots, cut up

1/4 cup gummy pine buds
1 handful dried hops

Put all in a pail of water and let stand overnight. The next morning, boil the mixture 2 or 3 hours, adding water when it boils too low. Strain the liquid into a crock, stir in 1-1/2 pints molasses and 2 quarts water. Put in 2 cakes of yeast dissolved in 1 cup cold water. Set the crock in a warm place while it ferments. When the top is covered with a thick, dark foam, skim off the foam and pour the liquid into clean bottles. Be careful not to disturb the sediment in the crock. Cork the bottles and set in a cool place. Will be ready to use in 2 days. Save the sediment to ferment the next brewing.

DANDELION WINE

Pick the heads of full-blown dandelion flowers. To one gallon flower heads add 1 gallon water, 2 oranges and their juice, the juice of 1 lemon and 1 oz. of crushed ginger root tied in a cloth bag. Put the flower heads and other ingredients in a pan and boil together 20 minutes. Strain and add 8 cups sugar. If the liquid is not clear, beat the white of an egg and add. Spread 1/2 oz. yeast on a slice of rye bread, float the bread on top of the liquid and leave the wine to work for a week. Strain and bottle. Cap the bottles loosely and tighten the caps after about a week. Best if seasoned 6 months before using.

EASY GRAPE JUICE

Select well-flavored grapes (Concords are very good), ripe but free of mold. Wash and stem the fruit. Place 1 heaping cupful of grapes into a hot, sterilized quart jar with 1/2 cup sugar. Fill each jar to within 1/2 inch of the top with boiling water and process 10 minutes in a boiling water bath. Store in a cool place for 6 weeks before using. Use the grapes from the jar as a garnish.

MEAD

A drink that goes all the way back to the Vikings!

water
5 lbs. honey
2 ozs. hops
2 ozs. coriander seeds

peels of 4 lemons
peels of 4 oranges
brandy

Heat the water almost to boiling, add the honey, stir to dissolve and then boil 1-1/2 hours. As soon as the scum forms, skim it off and continue to skim the liquid during cooking. Tie the hops and coriander seeds in separate cloth bags; add the bags and the lemon and orange peels to the honey syrup, remove from the heat and allow to cool. When cool, mix in a bottle of brandy and pour the liquid into a container which can be covered closely. Let stand 6 to 9 months before sampling; if you prefer a dryer mead, let it stand a few months longer.

MOCK MEAD

4 lbs. brown sugar (about 9 cups)
1 cup molasses
3 quarts boiling water
4 ozs. cream of tartar

1 oz. checkerberry or
   wintergreen leaves
1 oz. sassafras root

Mix brown sugar, molasses and boiling water and let cool to lukewarm. Add cream of tartar and let stand until cold. Add checkerberry or wintergreen and sassafras. Mix 2 tablespoons of this mixture in a glass of water with 1/3 teaspoon soda and serve with ice. Store any unused mead in a closed bottle in the refrigerator.

OLD COLONIAL PUNCH

1/2 lb. raisins
1 cup currants
1 quart boiling water
1 teaspoon almond extract
1/2 cup preserved ginger
juice of 4 oranges

juice of 2 lemons
2 cups confectioners' sugar
3 tablespoons grated coconut
1/2 teaspoon ground cinnamon
1 quart chilled ginger ale

Steep the raisins and currants in the boiling water for 30 minutes, strain and let cool. Add the almond extract, ginger, fruit juices, sugar, coconut and cinnamon. Mix together and chill. Pour in the chilled ginger ale just before serving and serve over crushed ice.

RHUBARB JULEP

Wash rhubarb stalks and cut them into 1-inch pieces. In a large pan, barely cover the rhubarb with water and boil moderately until the fruit is mushy and soft. Strain the cooked fruit; for a clear liquid, do not stir the fruit while it is draining. To each quart of the warm juice, add 1/2 cup sugar. Serve this juice alone or mix it with cranberry, orange or pineapple juice, or with ginger ale.

Syrups

MINT SYRUP

A nice addition to lemonade, iced tea or pineapple juice

2-1/2 cups sugar
1 cup water

20 stalks fresh mint, pounded

Combine ingredients in saucepan and stir over heat until the sugar dissolves. Simmer 15 minutes and strain. Pour into a jar and seal, storing in a cool place. Makes 2 cups syrup.

PEACH BLOSSOM NECTAR

Use this syrup with fruit juices or in hot tea or cold milk.

Gather 4 quarts peach blossoms when they are dewy fresh and clean and allow to dry. Cover the blossoms with boiling water and let stand for 24 hours. Strain off the liquid and pour it over 4 quarts more fresh blossoms, prepared as the first batch. After another 24 hours, strain the liquid and discard the used blossoms. Add 1 cup fresh blossoms and 1 cup sugar to each cup liquid. Boil this mixture until the syrup thickens, then strain and bottle.

SPICE SYRUP

Use in hot or iced tea instead of sugar.

2-1/2 cups sugar
1 cup water
2 tablespoons whole cloves

3 3-inch pieces stick cinnamon
1 small piece preserved ginger

Heat the ingredients together and strain. Use 1/4 cup with 6 cups of black or green tea.

SPRING TONIC

Administered as doses in the spring to clear the blood and stimulate the appetite. If you can't find burdock root or spikenard at the local natural food store, try a walk in the country with a naturalist and a spade.

1/4 lb. burdock root
1/2 lb. sarsaparilla root
1/4 lb. goldthread root
1/4 lb. dandelion root
1/4 lb. spikenard root

1/4 lb. red clover blossoms
1 handful hops
sugar
1 cup brandy

Brew the roots, clover blossoms and hops in a gallon of water for about an hour. Strain, add sugar to taste and stew down to a syrup. Add the brandy. To be taken as needed.